COSTUME

PHILLIS CUNNINGTON

A. & C. BLACK LTD
LONDON

01286

Black's Junior Reference Books

General Editor: R. J. Unstead

Acknowledgments

The drawings in this book are by the author, Miss Catherine Lucas, Cecil Everitt and Gay Galsworthy. Illustration 115 is from *English Costume of the 19th Century* by Iris Brooke. Illustration 69 is reproduced by gracious permission of Her Majesty the Queen. Grateful acknowledgment is also made to the following for permission to include portraits, photographs and drawings: His Grace the Duke of Rutland, 38; The Right Hon. the Earl Fitzwilliam, 41; Mr. Hardy Amies, 171; The Bodleian Library, 17 (ms. Bodley 764, fol. 41); Mrs. Peter Cazalet, 94; Sir Kenneth Clark, 58; the Essex Record Office, 39; Messrs. Faber & Faber Ltd., 15 (from *Handbook of English Mediaeval Costume*); 50 (from *Handbook of English Costume in the 16th Century*); 88 (from *Handbook of English Costume in the 18th Century*); 117, 131, 142 and 145 (from *Handbook of English Costume in the 19th Century*); and 112d, 135 and 136 (from *English Women's Clothing in the 19th Century*); King George VI Art Gallery, Port Elizabeth, 133; Mr. Miles Hadfield, 110; Miss Catherine Lucas, 120 and 175; National Portrait Gallery, 57 and 59; *Punch*, 165; *The Tailor and Cutter*, 156, 157 and 158; Tryon Palace Restoration, South Carolina, 96. For the fashions on page 62, grateful acknowledgment is made to Associated Newspapers Group Ltd.

Published by A & C Black (Publishers) Limited, 35 Bedford Row, London WC1R4JH
Reprinted 1982
ISBN 0-7136-0104-3

Printed and bound in Great Britain by BAS Printers Limited, Over Wallop, Hampshire

CONTENTS

A school boy from Reading
(1816)

13th Century

INTRODUCTION

This is the story of clothes worn by English people from the reign of Alfred the Great to Elizabeth II. In the early Middle Ages clothes were loose and simple. Everything had to be made by hand—there were, of course, no sewing machines, and even needles were very precious. Steel needles mostly had to be imported which added to their cost. Silver needles were also used. The poet Chaucer in the 14th century wrote:

> "with a thread basting (tacking) my sleeves" using "a silver needle".

By the laborious process of hand-spinning and hand-weaving various kinds of cloth were made. Peasants wore chiefly woollen clothes; the rich might have linen or silk. Cotton was not used in England until the 17th century and man-made fibres not until the 20th.

15th Century

When people learned to knit, in Queen Mary's reign, it was much easier to make fitting clothes such as stockings and tights. As time went on, more inventions helped tailors to get a better fit, and dressmakers revelled in the invention of the sewing machine, which came into general use in the 1850's. Elastic, too, which began to be used for clothes in 1830, was very welcome.

But do you ever wonder why we wear clothes at all and what they mean? Of course we need them for decency and, in our climate, for warmth. But quite apart from their practical uses, clothes can have special meanings.

17th Century

4

For example, the clothes of men and women are different, and this helps to make them attractive to each other. Again, clothes can be what is known as a "status symbol". Grand clothes distinguished a king or a nobleman from an ordinary person. Colours, too, often mean something. In the 17th century blue was worn by serving men and so was avoided by gentlemen. Scarlet often distinguished a judge and purple represented royalty. Even now, white suggests a wedding and black a funeral. In other ways clothes of a certain pattern, such as soldiers' uniforms, tell us that the wearers belong to a special group and are outside the ordinary fashion of the day.

Then why do fashions change? Partly because no one likes monotony but chiefly perhaps because to some extent clothes are bound to reflect ideas and ways of life that change with time.

A word about the pictures—you will notice that some of the people look unnatural. This is because the illustrations are all copied from pictures made at the actual times they represent. The medieval artist could be very highly skilled but he did not often study anatomy, so his figures sometimes look odd.

Then in the later parts of the book, fashion plates have sometimes been copied, and here the artists cared only about the clothes and often drew the people stiffly. The advantage of all the pictures is that you can be sure they show you the true fashions of the day, better than if they were drawn from imagination.

18th Century

19th Century

20th Century

5

9th to 11th CENTURIES

1. *Short belted tunic and pointed cap* (11th century)

MEN'S COSTUME

In the 9th century, that is during King Alfred's reign, and also in the 10th and 11th centuries, a man's suit consisted of a tunic and super-tunic.

The *tunic* was a sack-like garment generally put on over the head and worn next to the shirt. It might be long to the ankles or short to the knees. Boys' tunics were usually short. The sleeves were long and a belt was worn round the waist. This was useful for hitching up the tunic when a man was doing anything active, such as climbing fruit trees or wrestling.

The *super-tunic* (see picture 4) was worn over the tunic, probably for warmth, but it was not an outdoor garment. It had loose sleeves, but otherwise was shaped like the tunic, and both were sometimes embroidered when worn by noblemen.

2. *Tunic, short stockings, sword* (11th century)

3. *Cloak, short tunic, criss-cross leg bandages* (11th century)

4. *Long super-tunic over long tunic* (11th century)

5a. *Stockings with ornamental tops*

5b. *Criss-cross leg bandages* (11th century)

Out of doors a cloak was worn and often a little pointed cap, like the one in the first picture.

On their legs men wore loose underpants called *braies* (braies of the 13th century are shown in picture 6). Short stockings were sometimes worn, but leg bandages were popular, and noblemen wore them criss-cross up the leg.

Shoes were of leather or skin, and were often slit up the front and fastened with a thong or strap of leather round the ankle.

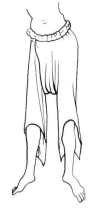

6. *Braies held up by a running string at the waist hem* (13th century)

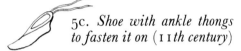

5c. *Shoe with ankle thongs to fasten it on* (11th century)

WOMEN'S COSTUME

Like the men, women wore a tunic and super-tunic, although the tunic or main garment was soon called a *kirtle*. These were always long, and their tight sleeves are shown in this picture. The super-tunic often had a sash-like girdle and rather wide sleeves. Tunics and super-tunics of grand ladies were generally embroidered.

On their heads, indoors and out, women wore a *veil*. This was a long broad scarf which covered the head completely, hiding the hair, and hung down over the shoulders. Queens even wore the veil under their crowns. It seems surprising that all through history until quite recent times, women practically always wore something on their heads, indoors as well as out.

Out of doors women wore cloaks similar to those worn by men.

7. *Lady in tunic, super-tunic, mantle and veil* (10th–11th century)

12th and 13th CENTURIES

8. *Short tunic or cote with front slit up. Hat worn over coif (13th century)*

MEN'S COSTUME

In the 12th and 13th centuries garments became shorter, and in the 13th century the tunic began to be called a *cote* and the super-tunic a *surcote*. Both were often slit up in the front, which must have made them easier to walk and to ride in. Often the surcote was sleeveless.

Out of doors cloaks were still worn and various forms of headgear. The pointed cap continued for a time, but men now often wore what was called a *coif*. This was a small, close-fitted linen cap tied under the chin. Over this could be worn a soft-pointed hood with a cape. In picture 11 one of the men on the top of the wall wears his hood over his head and the right-hand man below has thrown the hood back and shows his coif.

9a. *Brown, sleeveless surcote over blue cote. Chaplet worn over coif*
  b. *Dark blue and red surcote. Green coif*
  c. *Brown surcote with sleeves (about 1230)*

10. *Round hats, long tunics and cloaks (13th century)*

8

11. *Workmen in short cotes with coifs and hoods (13th century)*

12. *Short tunic or cote, cloak and coif (13th century)*

13. *Wrestlers showing braies. One is wearing long hose with straps under the feet. Coifs on head (about 1250)*

In the 13th century small round hats or caps with a "stalk" were very popular. Men often went barefoot, but stockings called *hose*, if worn, were made long enough to be pulled up over the braies as in picture 13. Often the hose had no feet, only under-instep straps.

9

14. *Thieves in short cotes, breaking into a church* (1125-1150)

Some hose were soled with leather so that separate shoes or boots need not be worn (see the man on a ladder in picture 14). It is recorded that King John had a pair made of cow-hide.

WOMEN'S COSTUME

15. *Kirtle with train (13th century)*

Women's clothes changed little until the 13th century. Their kirtles then often had trains; even the milkmaid in picture 17 wears a dress that must have swept the ground.

As before, cloaks were worn out of doors, and these were sometimes used inside the home as dressing-gowns. Henry III gave his sister Isobel "two scarlet cloaks, one lined with fur and another with silk to be used when she rose at night".

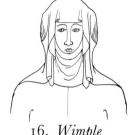

16. *Wimple*

In Henry II's reign (1154–1189) women began to wear a *wimple*; something like this is still worn by some nuns. It was a length of linen or silk, swathed round the chin and pinned to the hair above the ears under the veil (picture 16).

The favourite head-dress all through the 13th and into the 14th century was perhaps the *barbette and fillet*. It was made up of two stiff linen bands, the fillet worn round the head like a crown, the barbette going over the head and under the chin (picture 17). Although the head was covered up, some grand ladies wore their hair in two long plaits, often braided with ribbon. Only young girls might wear their hair flowing loose. Aristocratic ladies sometimes used make-up, including rouge, to enhance their beauty.

17. *Milkmaid in long kirtle; on her head a barbette and fillet (13th century)*

11

18. *Peasant in large hat and boots, still wearing a loose cote and surcote* (1340)

MEN'S COSTUME

In the 14th century country folk went on wearing loose cotes and surcotes.

Instead of the cote, gentlemen now began to wear a short close-fitting garment—a *gipon*, later called a *doublet*. It was buttoned or laced down the front and the belt was worn round the hips (picture 19).

There were several varieties of overgarment, one of which was the *cote-hardie* and another the *gown*. The cote-hardie can be recognised by the sleeves, which were short with long streamers called *tippets* hanging down from the elbow (picture 20). The gown, introduced in Richard II's reign, was wide, loose, and long when worn on ceremonial occasions. The sleeves were baggy and hung down from the wrists.

Out of doors capes or cloaks were worn. The ceremonial cloak was called a *mantle*.

19. *Doublet, mantle and long hose (about 1350)*

20. *A cote-hardie. The hood is thrown back (14th century)*

21. *Gown with "bag-pipe" sleeves, tall hat (late 14th century)*

22. *Cape over doublet. Hood and long hose (about 1350)*

Long tight hose were still worn and often the two legs were of different colours. This fashion lasted from the middle of the 14th century for about a hundred years.

Shoes with long pointed toes, like "winkle-pickers", were very fashionable from about 1370 to 1410, and again from 1460 to 1480. They were stuffed with moss, hay or tow, in order to keep this shape. Peasants and countrymen wore large loose leather boots with square toes like those in picture 18.

Men wore hats and some of these were trimmed with ostrich feathers. This was the first time that Englishmen had worn feathered hats. As to the hood, the point at the back was lengthened into a long streamer called a *liripipe*, shown in a rather exaggerated form in picture 24. An alternative head-dress to the hood was the *chaperon*, shown above in picture 23a.

23a. *Short gown, chaperon on head, hose of two different colours*
b. *Feather-trimmed hat, fur-lined mantle, pointed shoes (14th century)*

25. *Ceremonial mantle over doublet. Long tight hose, pointed (piked) shoes (14th century)*

24. *Hoods with long liripipes (late 14th century)*

13

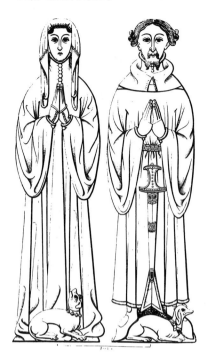

26. *Man and woman in similar gowns. The man has the cape of his hood turned down over his neck. The lady wears a veil (late 14th century)*

WOMEN'S COSTUME

Picture 26 shows that women wore gowns almost exactly like those worn by men. In the middle of the century a new overgarment came into fashion, called a *sideless surcote*. It was sleeveless, cut away under the arms, showing the kirtle underneath. Cloaks with hoods were worn for travelling or riding.

The wimple and veil were still worn, and the hair underneath was dressed in plaits turned up over the ears as in picture 27.

Shoes were like the men's and stockings were often scarlet.

27. *Veil, wimple and upright plaits of hair each side (14th century)*

28. *Lady in a sideless surcote, wearing a barbette and fillet. Man in long cote and hood. Youths in short cotes (14th century)*

15th CENTURY

MEN'S COSTUME

From the 15th century onwards the belt of the doublet was worn round the waist instead of at hip level. In different forms, the doublet was the man's chief body garment until the reign of Charles II, in the middle of the 17th century.

Over the doublet men could wear a cote-hardie, a *jacket* or a gown. The man in the middle of picture 29 is wearing a jacket, which was shaped like the doublet except for having "hanging sleeves". These were long enough for a man to fold round his hands to keep them warm. There was an opening part-way down the sleeve for putting the arm through, so that he could use his hands conveniently; the rest of the sleeve would then hang straight down.

29a. *Jacket with hanging sleeves*
b. *Gown with hanging sleeves*
(late 15th century)

The man on the far right is wearing a gown, which also has hanging sleeves. This garment was the fore-runner of the academic gown still worn by some teachers, and others, today.

The hose now reached right up to the waist. Rich people would have a manservant to help them to dress and here is a description of his duties written at the time:

30. *Short doublet, long tight hose and a small round cap (late 15th century)*

> "In the morning against your lord shall rise, take care that his linen be clean, and warm it at a clear fire. . . . Then pray your lord in humble words to come to a good fire and array him thereby. . . . First hold out to him his shirt, then his doublet while he puts in his arms . . . also his vamps (ankle-socks) and so shall he go warm all day. Thus draw on his hose and his socks by the fire, and lace or buckle his shoes, lace his doublet in every hole and put round his neck

*31. Lady in a cote-
hardie (15th century)*

and on his shoulders a kerchief and then gently comb his head with an ivory comb and give him water wherewith to wash his face. Then kneel down and say thus 'Sir, what robe or gown doth it please you to wear today?' Do on his girdle, arrange his robe in the proper fashion, give him a hood or hat for his head, a cloak or cappe-de-buse (cape) according as it be fair or foul or all misty with rain; and so shall ye please him."

WOMEN'S COSTUME

In the 15th century the kirtle was always covered by an overgarment, which might be a cote-hardie, with similar sleeves to those of the men; or, as before, a sideless surcote, showing the kirtle underneath; or lastly a gown.

*32. A sideless surcote worn
over kirtle. Note kirtle sleeves
(1403)*

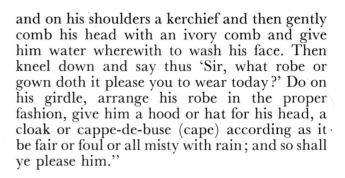
*33. Ladies in gowns and
heart-shaped head-dresses
(late 15th century)*

34. *Horned head-dress and templets*
(1416)

35. *Padded ring worn over a veil (early 15th century)*

36. *Steeple head-dress without the point (late 15th century)*

The gown was long, with wide, but not hanging, sleeves. It was worn with a belt and was rather short-waisted, as you can see in picture 33.

Women's head-dresses became very elaborate. They were evidently thought much more decorative than the hair. At first a padded ring was worn, as in picture 35. This was later bent up sideways to make a heart-shaped head-dress as you see on the women in picture 33.

The horned head-dress was the most elaborate. Picture 34 shows this kind; it also shows jewelled ornaments called *templets* in which ladies concealed their hair.

The tallest head-dress was like a steeple with the tip cut off. (It came from France where it was truly steeple-shaped.) The veil flowed down behind from the summit.

Last of all there was the popular "butterfly" head-dress. Here the veil was wired up to look like wings which, in a wind, must have behaved like sails!

37. *Butterfly head-dress*
(1482)

16th CENTURY

Men's Costume

A great change took place in men's and women's fashions during the Tudor period.

Men's clothes were puffed out with padding called *bombast*, which might be wool, flock, horsehair or rags. This tended to make all men appear very broad, like Henry VIII in picture 38. Their clothes, too, were often decorated with embroidery or with slashing. Through the slashes could be seen either the white shirt or a brightly coloured lining. Colours were usually bright, the most popular being scarlet and green.

A gentleman now had more clothes in his wardrobe.

38. *Henry VIII in doublet, short gown, flat cap and broad shoes (early 16th century)*

39. *Doublet with wings. Trunk hose (about 1595)*

He still wore a doublet which was padded and buttoned, hooked or tied down the front.

Stiff ornamental bands called *wings* surrounding the shoulder seams were generally added.

At the neck there was either a turned-down collar or a ruff. The collar was called a *falling band* (band was the word used for any sort of collar). Sir John Petre in picture 39 is wearing both falling band and ruff. The *ruff* was very fashionable in Queen Elizabeth's reign. It was a starched, tightly gathered frill, which stuck out all round the neck. You can still see small ruffs worn by choir boys today.

40. *Jerkins with wings and hanging sleeves* (1569)

41. *Sleeveless jerkin with wings. A doublet is worn underneath but only the sleeves show* (1568)

42. *Long gown with hanging sleeves* ((1538)

The jacket, soon to be called a *jerkin*, was worn over the doublet. It had either hanging sleeves or wings only.

A man wore a gown, like the 15th-century gown, over his doublet and jerkin on special occasions. This must have been uncomfortably warm at times: for a little later on, it is recorded that Charles I's brother, Prince Henry, flung off his gown at a dance.

In Elizabeth I's reign, the gown's hanging sleeves became sham, and remained as ornamental flat strips dangling from the arm-hole seam. These strips are still worn on the gowns of the Wandsmen (vergers) at St. Paul's Cathedral and some other churches. Oddly enough in the next two centuries these strips on small children's dresses were used by mothers as reins and were called leading strings.

43. *Trunk hose with stockings pulled up over them. Short cloak and small cap called a bonnet* (1582)

44. *Trunk hose, very bulky* (1575)

Men continued to wear long hose or tights until 1550. These were made of soft material cut on the cross so as to get a good fit. They were so difficult to put on that this is what a man living at the time wrote:

"... the long seams of our hose be set by a plumb-line (straight), then we puff, then we blow, and finally sweat till we drop."

Dressing must have been very much easier when knitting was introduced in Queen Mary's reign (1553–1558) and knitted hose and stockings began to be worn. In her reign, too, men started wearing what were called *trunk hose*, in which the upper part was padded so as to bulge out all round. Sometimes the tight-fitting portions ended just above the knee with ordinary stockings pulled up over them as in picture 43.

A much more important change was introduced towards the end of Queen Elizabeth's reign, when *knee breeches* called Venetians came into fashion for the first time. They fastened below the knee. The man in picture 45 wears his stockings pulled up over them.

45. *Knee breeches and padded doublet. Buttons in left sleeve cover a space for a pocket handkerchief* (1590)

Out of doors cloaks of various kinds were worn.

46. *Flat cap* (1527)

Headgear varied. Henry VIII set a fashion for a *flat cap*. This had a flat crown spreading over the flat narrow brim. His own was trimmed with jewels and feathers. The flat cap was so popular with townsfolk that it came to be called "the city flat cap". Another kind of headgear was a small round brimless cap called a *bonnet* (see picture 43):

"Off goes his bonnet to an oyster wench."
(Shakespeare: *Richard II*. Act 1, Sc. 4.)

Hats, except for the straw hats chiefly worn by country folk, were uncommon until Elizabeth's reign. Then the *copotain hat*, with a tall crown and small brim, became very popular. Shakespeare mentions it in "The Taming of the Shrew":

47. *Copotain hat* (1575)

"O fine villain! A silken doublet, a velvet hose!
A scarlet cloak! And a copotain hat."
Shakespeare: *Shrew*. Act v, Sc. 1

48. *Broad shoes* (1539)

Shoes rather than boots were fashionable except for riding. In Henry VIII's reign the toes of shoes, instead of being pointed, were made so broad that a law was actually passed limiting the width of the toe to six inches.

WOMEN'S COSTUME

In Tudor times fashionable women's clothes became almost as elaborate as men's. The cote-hardie and surcote went out of fashion and the gown was the usual overgarment. This was open in front to show the ornamental kirtle underneath. Later in the century the kirtle became a *petticoat* only, and gradually the word "gown" came to mean a woman's dress in the modern sense.

49. *Gown open in front to show embroidered under-skirt. The gown is trimmed with aglets (metal ornaments) and the flat strips are the remains of hanging sleeves* (1562)

21

The style of sleeve you see Mary Tudor wearing in picture 50 went out of fashion in the reign of Queen Elizabeth, who probably did not like it as much as the new styles.

50. *Mary Tudor with a pomander* (*about* 1545)

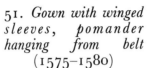

51. *Gown with winged sleeves, pomander hanging from belt* (1575–1580)

A most striking change took place in 1545, when women started wearing an underskirt called a *farthingale*. This was stiffened with hoops of wire or whalebone to make the skirt of the gown spread out from the waist, as in picture 52. Very large farthingales made the skirt so wide that it was impossible to come into a room through a narrow door, and someone at the time wrote:

> "Alas poor farthingales must lie in the street
> To house them no door in the city made meet
> Since at our narrow doors they in cannot win." (1599)

Many women, especially middle-class and working women, did not wear farthingales, and their general style of dress changed very little until the end of James I's reign.

When ruffs came into fashion for men, in the 1550's, women also wore them. Some liked them open in the front to show their necks or necklaces.

52. *Shows change in style of sleeves. Gown worn over a farthingale* (1592)

Out of doors cloaks were still worn, and sometimes mufflers. A *muffler* at this time was a square of material folded diagonally and tied over the mouth and nose as a protection from cold air. Gloves and muffs became fashionable.

A lady did not carry a handbag, so she often suspended from her belt, her purse, a mirror, a muff, a fan or a little case called a *pomander* (pictures 50 and 51) holding perfume or a charm against the common cold.

53. *English hood—early style (about 1501)*

Head-dresses were smaller than in the 15th century. The *English hood* was fashionable from 1500 to about 1540. It was stiffened in front to make a pointed arch above the forehead and hung down behind in a sort of curtain which could be pinned up to get it out of the way. At first the hair under the arch was visible, but soon it was enclosed in striped rolls as in picture 54. The *French hood*, which came into fashion a little later, was low, curving round the back of the head and showing much of the front hair. It had a stiff curtain behind which could be turned

54. *English hood—later style—with curtain turned up* (1536)

up and laid flat on the head to shade the face from the sun. The French hood had two jewelled bands following the curve of the hood. The *lettice cap* was a fur bonnet. By Elizabeth's reign tall-crowned hats, like the men's, were popular wear out of doors.

55. *French hood* (1540)

Women kept their stockings up by *garters* which were bands or sashes, often embroidered and tied below the knee. They are described in "The Lady Greensleeves":

> "Thy garters fringed with the gold and silver aglets (ornaments) hanging by." (1584)

56. *Lettice cap* (1527–1528)

Make-up with powder and paint was common and black *patches*, made of velvet or silk and stuck on the face to show the beauty of the complexion, began to be used at the end of the century. Like Queen Elizabeth, many ladies dyed their hair.

MEN'S COSTUME—EARLIER STYLES

In James I's reign there were few changes in men's fashions, except that trunk hose became very long and baggy.

When Charles I came to the throne in 1625 he discouraged padding and clothes became less bulky, but there was a rage for lace and ribbon trimmings. The Puritans' colours were usually dark. In fact black became fashionable for all gentlemen and the only really bright colour frequently worn was scarlet. Blue was avoided all through the century by the upper classes because by now it was the colour worn by servants and apprentices.

Men continued to wear doublets until 1670, but the jerkin went out of fashion soon after Charles I came to the throne. Men's doublets

57. Sir Walter Raleigh in trunk hose and son, aged eight, in breeches (1602)

58. Doublet with sleeves slashed down the front seam. Long breeches. Wide "falling band" or collar (1635–1645)

59. Charles I in doublet and breeches. Top boots (1631)

24

varied a good deal, as you can see by comparing pictures 57, 58, and 59. The shape of the sleeves changed too, and slashing gradually went out of fashion except for one slit down the front seam.

The gown, with its hanging sleeves, was soon given up by ordinary men, but was still worn by members of the learned professions such as University men, lawyers, etc.

As in the previous century, instead of a ruff, a man could wear a falling band. All through the 1630's the falling band was wide, spreading from side to side and often edged with lace.

Instead of bulbous trunk hose, knee breeches became the rule. There were several new styles of breeches. Two of them are shown in pictures 58 and 59.

60. *Gown with hanging sleeves* (1668)

61. *Dutch breeches, trimmed with ribbon* (*about* 1650)

62. *Charles II wearing petticoat breeches and top boots with boot hose tops. He holds a "cavalier hat"* (1662)

A third style (*Dutch breeches*), looking rather like shorts, are shown in picture 61. *Petticoat breeches* were like a very full divided skirt to the knees (picture 62). They were trimmed with ribbon, and in some cases up to 250 yards of ribbon were used. Charles II, returning from France in 1660, supported this fashion in England, but Englishmen so disliked it that it lasted only about ten years.

Out of doors cloaks were still the fashion. Hats with wide brims, some trimmed with feathers, were also worn indoors, especially on formal occasions. Pepys wrote in his diary in 1661:

> "Got a strange cold in my head by flinging off my hat at dinner."

Men's hair was curled and long to the shoulders. Some men were clean shaven, others wore a pointed beard.

63. Guy Fawkes wearing cloak, top boots and spurs (1605)

64. Shoe roses, long curled hair, feather-trimmed hat

For the first time, men's boots and shoes began to have high heels. Red heels were worn on grand occasions. A remarkable decoration was the *shoe rose*, a huge rosette of ribbon or lace (picture 64). Men wore long boots with wide tops and spurs, whether on foot or riding.

With Charles II the colours of men's stockings generally became gayer, and they could be green, yellow or even scarlet. Dandies sometimes wore false calves inside their stockings to improve the shape of their legs.

To prevent the leather of the boots from staining the stockings, boots were lined with an extra pair of stockings. The tops of these were turned down over the tops of the boots as an elegant lace-edged frill (*boot hose tops*).

65. Boot hose tops (about 1635)

66. *Puritan in cloak, plain hat and falling band (1676)*

67. *Smart youth in feather-trimmed hat. Coat of latest fashion and cravat. Note sword and cane (1676)*

68. *Overcoat, sword (1689)*

MEN'S COSTUME—LATER STYLES

Near the end of Charles II's reign, a great change took place. Doublets were discarded and a man's suit consisted of *coat, waistcoat,* and *breeches.* This was really the beginning of modern dress. The coat hung down to the knees; it had no collar and the sleeves had deep turn-back cuffs.

A neckcloth of muslin called a *cravat* was tied round the neck. The ends, edged with lace, were left dangling. A square turn-down collar was also worn, especially by Puritans.

The waistcoat, although it was worn under the coat, had sleeves. The breeches were rather full.

Out of doors, cloaks (still worn by the Puritan in picture 66) began to be replaced by overcoats as in picture 68. Swords were still worn by gentlemen as a mark of distinction.

Children wore clothes like those of their parents, except that boys, even to the age of eight (like Charles II's brother in picture 69), were dressed like their sisters.

69. *Charles II's brother aged eight years and dressed like a girl (1647)*

27

WOMEN'S COSTUME

Women's fashions did not change very much until the reign of Charles I (1625–1649). Until then grand ladies continued to wear dresses with skirts spread out over wide farthingales but these then went out of fashion.

In the new style of dress the bodice was low-necked and the long, full skirt hung straight down. It was still sometimes open in front to show an underskirt.

A favourite kind of sleeve was pulled in round the elbow and slashed and puffed out above and below, as in picture 71. Others were wide with broad cuffs.

70. *Gentleman in doublet, trunk hose, cloak and plumed hat. Lady wearing a wide farthingale and gown with hanging sleeves (1613)*

72. *Sleeves with turned-back cuffs. Child wearing a coif and a turn-down collar or falling band (1649)*

For neckwear women had a choice between ruffs and collars. Women alone wore ruffs that were oval in shape. All ruffs went out of fashion by 1650. Collars might be fan shaped, standing up round the back of the neck as in picture 70, or turned down like the child's in picture 72.

71. *Oval ruff. 'Virago' sleeves (1630)*

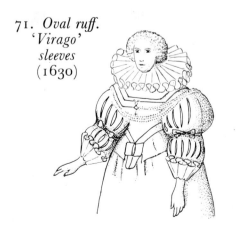

28

73. *Lady wearing an overcoat, hood and mask* (1640)

74. *Neckerchief, large hat worn over coif, and muff* (1640)

75. *Neckerchief worn indoors, and coif* (1640)

Out of doors cloaks, capes, *overcoats* and *neckerchiefs* were all worn by women and they also carried *muffs*. The neckerchief was a large folded square, worn over the shoulders but otherwise like the head-square of today. It was also worn indoors.

Women had large hats like those of the men, and *coifs* were ordinarily worn indoors.

76. *Large hat. Falling ruff* (about 1627)

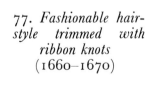

77. *Fashionable hair-style trimmed with ribbon knots* (1660–1670)

On dressy occasions women wore ribbon bows called knots, as hair ornaments. The *top knot* was a large bow worn on the top of the head. Remember the nursery rhyme which said:

"The wind shall blow my top knot off."

29

78. *Back and front views of fontange* (1699)

79a. *Country woman on pattens. She wears a neckerchief* (1640)

79b. *Close-up of a 17th-century patten*

In the last ten years of the century, the *fontange* came into fashion. This was an indoor linen cap with a small flat crown behind and a tall erection of lace or lace and linen frills in front, kept erect by a wire frame. Two long lace or linen streamers called "lappets" hung down at the back or were sometimes pinned up to the crown.

Pattens, shown in pictures 79a and b, were wooden soles raised on iron rings. They were kept on by straps and worn with ordinary shoes, chiefly by country women to keep them out of the mud, since roads at that time were not "made up". High heels came into fashion, and they were often made of cork for lightness. Girls were very proud of them:

> "I came trip trip over the Market Hill, holding up my petticoats to the calves of my legs, to show my fine coloured stockings, and how trimly I could foot it in a new pair of corked shoes I had bought." (1623)

Make-up with paint, powder and patches continued. Far from liking to be sunburnt as most girls do today, women often protected their faces by *masks*. Such a mask was also sometimes worn as a disguise. Pepys in his diary, calls it a vizard:

> "She put on her vizard and so kept it on all the Play which of late is become a great fashion among the ladies, which hides their whole face." (12th June 1663)

80. *Mask* (17th century)

18th CENTURY

MEN'S COSTUME

All through the 18th century men's clothes were much less complicated than in the 17th. Everyone wore coat, waistcoat and, until the end of the century, knee breeches. From 1790 men took to wearing tights called *pantaloons*. There is a picture of these on the next page.

At first there was only one style of coat. This was close-fitting to the waist and then flared out to just below the knees. The sleeves generally had heavy, turned-back cuffs or just slits at the wrist. This type of coat had no collar until about 1765; then a stand-up collar was added.

81. *Father and son in fashionable coats and waistcoats and wearing wigs. Daughter wears a "pinner" on her head* (1741)

All through the Georgian period the front of the coat was gradually curved further and further back till by the end of the century it had become a *tail coat*.

Men often found their tightly fitting clothes uncomfortable, and so, in 1730, a loose coat with a flat turn-down collar came into fashion for alternative wear. This coat, which in pictures you can recognise by its turn-down collar, was called a *frock*. An English gentleman writing from Paris in 1752 said:

"I was so damned uneasy in a full-dressed coat . . . I frequently sighed for my little loose frock."

82. *Coat with stand-up collar, turned-back cuffs* (1766)

83. *Frock with sleeves slit up from wrist instead of a cuff* (1735)

31

84. *Banyan and night-cap* (1735)

Another comfortable coat was the one sometimes called a *nightgown*, or a *banyan*. The term nightgown is confusing as it was not worn in bed; the term banyan came from India.

The waistcoat was made much like the coat until in the middle of the century its sleeves disappeared. As the coat became more open in front, the waistcoat grew shorter.

86. *Frock, short waistcoat, tricorne hat, stock at neck* (1777)

87. *Both men wear pantaloons with buttoned flaps and round hats. (b) wears a spencer over his coat and muffler over his mouth (about 1795)*

85. *Coat, long waistcoat, stockings rolled over breeches. At the neck, a cravat. He wears a wig and carries a sword* (1720)

Round their necks men either continued to wear *cravats* (picture 85) or else *stocks* (picture 86). The stock was a high made-up collar, tied or buckled behind and stiffened with cardboard. One poor gentleman complained:

"My neck is stretched out in such a manner that I am apprehensive of having my throat cut with the paste board." (1761)

88. *Dr. Johnson wearing a greatcoat, tricorne hat, large bushy wig and top boots* (1773)

Breeches were buckled below the knee and generally closed in front by buttoned flaps, as were pantaloons. They were kept up by tightening the waistband until about 1787 when braces, known as *gallowses*, were introduced. For nearly half the century stockings were pulled up over the knees of the breeches and called *rollups*. Only afterwards were the breeches buckled over the stockings.

Workmen and little boys were the first to wear *trousers*. The young boy in picture 89 is wearing them.

Out of doors men wore a *greatcoat*, which was loose with a large turn-down collar. A popular name for it was a "wrap rascal". At the extreme end of the century a very short-waisted jacket called a *spencer* was introduced for outdoor wear (picture 87).

A hat with the brim turned up so as to make it three-cornered (later called a *tricorne*) lasted all through the 18th century. Even little boys wore them. In the schoolroom picture below you can see their tricornes hanging on the wall. Towards the end of the century there was an alternative hat called the *round hat*, like the boy's in picture 89.

89. *Boy in round hat, overcoat and skeleton suit* (1790) (See page 53 for description of skeleton suit)

90. *Schoolmaster and boys, their tricorne hats hanging up* (about 1770)

33

Nightcaps, soft and shaped something like round tea-cosies, made of linen or velvet, were worn with "nightgowns" indoors, covering the shaved head when the wig was removed. Woollen nightcaps were worn in bed.

91.
Night-cap

Wigs were the fashion all through the century. The variety of wigs was enormous and some kinds were even worn by working men.

92a. *Catogan or club wig (about 1770)*

b. *Physical wig (1787)*

c. *Major wig (1750-1800)*

d. *Pigtail wig (1779)*

e. *Full bottom wig (about 1700)*

On their feet, men wore either shoes with large buckles or top boots. Fashionable men used powder and rouge and we are told that even now "the grand distinguishing mark of a fine gentleman is the wearing of a sword".

93. *Top boot*

94. *Frocks, waistcoats and breeches. Both men have tricorne hats and buckled shoes (1760)*

However, sticks called *canes* were also smart, and young men started carrying them instead of swords, as you saw in picture 86. Jonas Hanway introduced umbrellas into England in 1756, but these strange novelties were not very popular for some time.

The colours in this century were rather softer than in the last, and blue could now be worn by gentlemen.

Women's dresses were mainly of two kinds, which can best be described as open and closed robes. The *open robe* had a bodice and skirt joined at the waist, but the skirt was open in front showing a decorated under-skirt called a *petticoat*. (A petticoat in the 18th century was not an undergarment, but the name for a skirt.) The "wrapping gown" was also open but was wrapped over in front. The *closed robe* had, of course, no opening in the skirt—see the doll in picture 96.

95. *A wrapping gown*
(1740–1750)

96. *Child in mob cap. Doll in closed robe with stomacher front to bodice (about 1760)*

The most celebrated of the dresses of this time was the *sack back gown* (open or closed), generally known as the sack. This had a double box pleat spreading down the back from neck to hem. It went out of fashion in 1780.

97. *Sack back gown. Stomacher front to bodice (about 1760)*

35

Some dresses had separate bodices and skirts, the bodice being in the form of a short jacket. Fancy aprons without bibs were often worn as an added decoration to the dress and not as protection. A very transparent one is shown in picture 99.

All the gowns had low necks and some bodices were open in front, the space being filled in by an ornamental panel called a *stomacher*. Sleeves were elbow length till the last quarter of this century and finished with a turned-back cuff or with deep flounces called *ruffles*.

The striking feature at this time was the hang of the skirt. Until about 1780 *hoop* petticoats, often just called hoops, were the fashion.

98. Jacket and skirt style, skirt over domed hoop (1718–1720)

99. Open robe, over oblong hoop. Transparent apron. Stomacher front to bodice. This lady wears a round-eared cap and holds a bergère hat (1743–1745)

The hoop was an under petticoat spread out on hoops of cane, wire or whalebone. The favourite shapes were the domed or bell shaped (picture 98) and the oblong (picture 99).

The oblong hoop was oval, spreading out enormously on each side. It lasted from 1740 till 1760 in spite of being very inconvenient. It was sometimes so wide that ladies had to bend it up under the arms in order to get through a narrow door.

The fashion for hoops went out after 1780 except at Court, where they were worn till 1820. That year George IV came to the throne and, as he did not like hoops, Court ladies stopped wearing them.

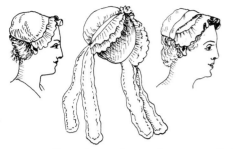

100. *Round-eared caps* (1730–1760)

White linen caps were worn indoors and the favourites were the *round-eared cap* and the *mob cap*. The mob cap had a puffed-up crown with a frilled border. Until 1750 it was bonnet shaped and could be tied under the chin with ties called "kissing strings".

101. *Bergère hat worn over coif* (1750–1760)

Women wore soft hoods or hats out of doors, generally on top of their caps. The most popular was a large straw hat with a low crown called the *bergère* (shepherdess) hat, because ladies had a fancy for looking countrified.

Hairstyles until the 1760's were fairly simple. Short ringlets at the back and sides were worn. These were often false and just pinned on. Strange to say, it was fashionable to powder the hair until it looked almost white.

102. *Mob cap with kissing strings* (1745)

103. *Schoolmistress in mob cap* (about 1770)

Ladies' shoes now had high heels and pointed toes, and they were tied or buckled over high tongues. Grand ladies' shoes were often made of crimson leather, brocade, silk or satin. Pattens were still worn by country folk.

104. *Lady's brocade shoe* (1740–1750)

Stockings of yarn, worsted or silk, were brightly coloured—blue, pink, green and especially scarlet being favourite colours.

Make-up in the 18th century was very elaborate among the upper classes. Rouge and even white paint might be applied to the face. Lips and finger-nails were reddened; eyebrows were arched to the right shape or shaved off and replaced by artificial ones made of mouse skin. Black patches were still dotted about the face.

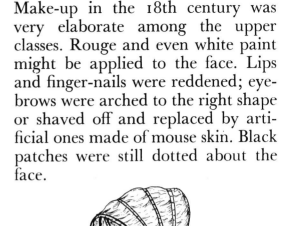

105. *Lady wearing a polonaise, pattens and, on her head, a calash* (1770–1780)

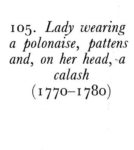

106. *Fashionable polonaise and high hair style* (1778)

WOMEN'S COSTUME—LATER STYLES

Soon after George III came to the throne in 1760, although most of the previous styles continued, some new styles came in. The *polonaise*, which came into fashion in the 1770's, was very popular. It was an open robe with the overskirt bunched up behind in several puffs. It was usually what was then considered short, showing the ankles, but sometimes it had a train.

Hairstyles were high, built up on pads and cushions. If a lady had not enough hair of her own, she bought a wig in the correct mode. This was written in a magazine of 1777:

"With Babel towers of hair as high
as if they meant to reach the sky."

To cover their heads on wet days women wore a large folding hood, built up on arches of whalebone or cane, looking rather like the hood of a baby's pram. It was called a *calash*. The lady in picture 105 is wearing one.

In the last six years of the century a tremendous change took place. Women aimed at having vertical outlines with nothing projecting anywhere. High waists and narrow skirts, often with trains, were now worn. The more sporting type of women preferred to wear a riding habit, but this too was high waisted and straight. It consisted of a short coat, a waistcoat and a long skirt.

a   *b*

107a. *High-waisted afternoon dress.* b. *High-waisted evening dress. Both ladies wear ostrich feathers and long gloves* (1799)

108. *Riding habits in green and blue. Round beaver caps* (1799)

Although this was intended for riding, it was also worn in England as a day dress, much to the surprise of foreigners.

Hair was now often cut short like a boy's, or arranged in short curls. Hats and bonnets were small.

For evening dress and Court wear, hair decorations were remarkable. Tall ostrich feathers worn upright were very popular. These could be rather embarrassing, as it was sometimes difficult to keep them standing up. Other curious decorations are described in one of Jane Austen's letters:

"Flowers are very much worn and fruit is still more the thing. Elizabeth has a bunch of strawberries and I have seen grapes, cherries, plums and apricots."

(1799)

19th CENTURY

MEN'S COSTUME

In the 19th century a gentleman had three different kinds of suit —his day suit, his dress suit and his sports wear.

His *day suit* consisted of coat, waistcoat and either trousers or pantaloons. During the first half of the 19th century the coat, waistcoat and trousers were often made of different materials and even different colours. The waistcoat, which was short, was often brightly coloured.

109a. Gentleman skating in brown overcoat, blue tail coat, yellow gloves and top hat

109b. Skater in blue tail coat, yellow pantaloons, yellow gloves and top hat (1815–1820)

110. Gardening in tail coat, strapped trousers and top hat (1833)

Until about 1840, at the beginning of Queen Victoria's reign, the day coat was either a tail coat, or a frock coat, or a morning coat.

The *tail coat* was like that of the 18th century, except that it was cut away squarely in front so that nothing was left below the waist except the tails behind. In fact, it was very like the formal evening dress coat of today; you may have seen this being worn by the conductor of an orchestra or the head waiter in a hotel.

The *frock coat* (quite different from the 18th-century "frock") was the most popular day coat from 1816 on, and all through Queen Victoria's reign.

The *morning coat* was a slightly more formal coat than the frock coat (it is still worn on such occasions as smart weddings and Court receptions). This was buttoned down the front to waist level and then the fronts curved away to the back, leaving a sort of rounded tail coat.

111. *Frock coat (about 1830)*

After about 1840 a gentleman could, for the first time, wear a comfortable short jacket like that of today, instead of the other coats.

In the first few years of the 19th century, breeches were often worn, but trousers soon became fashionable and have remained so ever since. *Strapped trousers* were worn from 1820 to about 1850. Each trouser leg was held down by a strap under the shoes or boots as in picture 110.

During the first half of the century a man could wear tights, called pantaloons, instead of trousers. These, when long, were also strapped under the instep as in picture 112, but they often ended above the ankle.

112. *Early style of morning coat, and strapped pantaloons* (1807)

41

A man's *dress suit* consisted of a tail coat, waistcoat and breeches or pantaloons, but after the 1840's trousers were worn. The coat could be any dark colour, blue being the favourite, but for the trousers black was correct. Right at the end of the century a dinner jacket, instead of the tail coat, was introduced for less formal evening wear.

For sport, short coats and knee breeches were worn all through the century. In the 1870's the Norfolk suit came into fashion. The *Norfolk jacket* had box pleats and a belt of the same material. It was worn with *knickerbockers* which were wide breeches gathered in below the knee.

113. *Evening dress*
a. *Blue coat, drab breeches, white stockings* (1807)

b. *Brown coat and waistcoat, pantaloons strapped inside the slippers* (1829)

114. *Norfolk suit. Homburg hat* (1876)

At first people thought them very ugly and, seeing a man wearing knickerbockers for the first time, a Parson wrote:

"... it is wonderful how men do disfigure their appearance nowadays." (1863)

At their necks men wore large bow ties or, from 1860, the *octagon tie*, which was a made-up tie, filling in the space between the neck and the waistcoat:

"With a hat all awry
And an octagon tie
And a miniature, miniature
glass in his eye."
(*Bab Ballads*)

115. *Bow tie* (1840–1850)

116. *Octagon tie* (1890)

117a. *Box coat with many capes.*
b. *Ordinary overcoat* (1812)

118. *Overcoat with one cape* (1869)

Besides the ordinary long greatcoat, there were several kinds of outdoor coats, all with capes. The *box coat* had several capes one on top of another, to shed the rain and keep one warm when driving, or travelling on top of a stage coach (see picture 117). The *Ulster*, very like the coat in picture 118, had only one cape. A special feature—a little pocket for a railway ticket in the sleeve just above the cuff— was added to it in 1875.

The *macintosh* appeared in 1836. It was a short, loose, supposedly waterproof overcoat made of india rubber cloth patented by Charles Macintosh. Unfortunately it had a horrible smell. This is what someone wrote about it:

> "A Mackintosh is now become a troublesome thing in town from the difficulty of their being admitted into an omnibus on account of the offensive stench which they emit."

At first the macintosh does not seem to have been altogether successful, as in 1837 Mr. Adam Black, the publisher, wrote:

> "My vaunted McIntosh travelling cape wet through and through."

As for men's headwear, the *top hat* with the chimney pot crown and narrow brim was the favourite. It was black and shiny and often called a silk hat.

119. *Macintosh and top hat* (1839)

The *bowler-hat* shape was worn as early as 1820, but the name did not come in until after 1850, when a Mr. William Bowler made "bowlers" popular with all classes. Although black was usual, brown or fawn bowlers were often worn with Norfolk jackets.

Straw hats, sailor hats called *boaters* (picture 120 shows them worn by men and women), peaked caps and *glengarries* were all worn in the country. *Homburg* hats, which were soft with a dent in the crown, began to be worn from the 1870's.

120. *Family group. The girl of fifteen wears a long dress, boots and a boater (about 1893)*

a. *Bowler* (1896)

b. *Deerstalker* (1890)

c. *Homburg* (1896)

d. *Lady's glengarry* (1864)

121. *Hats*

Men had given up wearing wigs long since and their hair was cut fairly short but, in Queen Victoria's reign, they took to wearing side whiskers with or without beards.

For footwear men wore slippers indoors with short toe-caps, and out of doors boots were the rule. *Wellington boots*, named after the Duke, became popular after 1817. These were high boots without a turn-over top. Short elastic-sided boots and button boots began to be fashionable when Queen Victoria came to the throne and these lasted till the end of her reign.

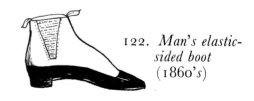

122. *Man's elastic-sided boot (1860's)*

Women's costume in the 19th century can be roughly divided into four periods:
1. The high-waisted period (often called the Regency period)
2. The wide-skirt-and-crinoline period
3. The bustle period
4. The practical period

123. People in Richmond Park. The ladies have high-waisted dresses and four wear poke bonnets. The kneeling gentleman has strapped trousers (1822)

1. The high-waisted period (1800 to about 1820)

During the "Regency period" skirts were at first long and often had trains; sleeves were long or short, but low necks and short sleeves were correct for evening dress. After the first ten years dresses got a little shorter.

Women went on wearing mob caps indoors during the day. Out of doors they wore hats or bonnets. These had wide brims, some of the bonnets poking forward, as in picture 123.

45

A gentleman once wrote complaining of these "poke bonnets":

> "Another street nuisance is your poke bonnet, ladies who sometimes put out your eyes with those penthouse projections or hook off your hat with their parasols. Some of them swing a velvet or satin bag as big as a postman's against your shins."   (1822)

124. *Tall bonnet* (1817)

125. *Tall evening dress head gear* (1817)

Some of the hats and bonnets were very tall and these, too, were laughed at. A man wrote in 1817:

> "Their head-dresses have grown to such a prodigious height that I am told that all the new houses have their doors reaching up to the ceilings."

Out walking, a lady could wear a high-waisted *pelisse*, which was now a long close-fitting overcoat as in picture 126, or she might prefer a cloak, a shawl, or a spencer. Spencers, like the men's, were very short jackets, ending at high waist level (picture 127).

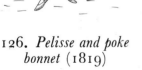

126. *Pelisse and poke bonnet* (1819)   **127.** *Spencer and poke bonnet* (1820)

2. *The wide-skirt-and-crinoline period* (1820's to 1870)

With these dresses the waist-line came down to the normal level. Women made the waist as small as possible by lacing up their stays very tightly. The skirt was at first widened with several petticoats, and in the 1830's the sleeves were like balloons.

Soon after Queen Victoria came to the throne in 1837, sleeves were less full, and often tight to the wrist. For evening dress they were short. The skirt, however, was made wider still by a petticoat made of a stiff material called *crinoline.*

128. *Maid wearing fashionable style of sleeves* (1827–1829)

129. *Fashionable dress of the period* (1834)

130. *Dress of figured lilac with sleeves fashionable at this time* (1839)

Finally in 1856 the "cage crinoline" was invented. It was held out on a frame of whalebone or fine wire, reminiscent of the 18th-century "hoop". The wired crinolines were light to wear but were often very awkward, especially when one sat down in an armchair. Although the height of fashion, they were very much laughed at, as picture 131 shows.

131. *This picture pokes fun at the very wide crinoline worn under the skirt* (1856)

132. *Evening dress of white tulle, trimmed with white and green beads* (1839)

About the same time an American lady called Mrs. Bloomer tried to persuade English women to give up wearing skirts and to wear instead loose trousers drawn in round the ankles and edged with a frill. They were nick-named *bloomers*. But no one liked them, and skirts of varying sizes and shapes were worn to the end of the century. In fact, clothes suitable for sport or any sort of exercise did not come into fashion

133. Crinolines were even worn on the beach (about 1864–1866)

until the end of Queen Victoria's reign. Ladies even wore crinolines on the beach, and, in the next period, played tennis in tight skirts with trains. Small white lace day caps were still worn indoors.

Out of doors women wore overcoats with spreading skirts or else large mantles or shawls, as in picture 137.

134. Ladies in wide crinolines and "spoon" bonnets. One wears a spreading overcoat (1865)

135. Lace cap (1874)

136. Pork pie hat (1866)

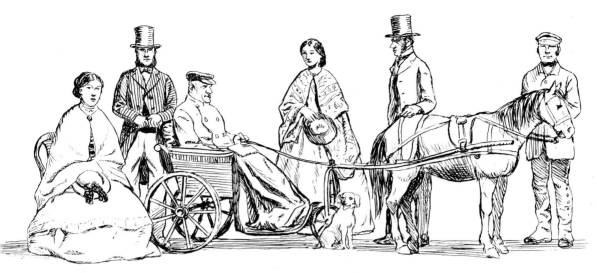

137. *Family group. Ladies have shawls and hats* (1860)

At first hats were wide and voluminously trimmed as on the right. Then small bonnets and little round hats, called from their shape *pork pie hats*, were favourites with young women. In the early 1860's many women wore *spoon bonnets*, so called because they looked like a spoon round the face. To shade the face an extra brim called an "ugly" could be added to this bonnet. The ugly was very like the front half of a calash. It could be folded up and put in the handbag when not required.(See picture 105.)

138. *Tall hat of early period* (1828)

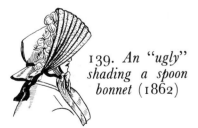

139. *An "ugly" shading a spoon bonnet* (1862)

Hairstyles were curly and high in the 1830's, but demure in the 1840's and 50's when the hair was usually smoothed down from a central parting to cover the ears and then twisted into a small bun behind. This was followed by a large bun called a *chignon* falling down the back of the neck, and generally enclosed in a thick black hair net.

Boots with coloured stockings were worn out of doors, but white stockings were more usual with shoes.

It was during this period that the sewing machine was invented and improved, making it much easier for dressmakers to tackle the very complicated dresses of the next period.

140. *Chignon* (1864)

3. *The bustle period* (about 1870–1890)

The true *bustle* was a large pad stuffed with wool, worn behind just below the waist, under the skirt, to puff it out. This now became so important, especially through the 1880's, that everyone rich or poor wore one, even if it had to be made out of dusters or newspaper. By the end of the period it bulged out so far that people said you could rest a tea-tray on it.

An outside patch pocket in the skirt came in as a new fashion. A magistrate was heard to remark:

> "Who in the name of all that's amazing designed the present custom of a pocket worn at the back and outside? There could not be a more convenient arrangement for a pick-pocket."   (1876)

141. *Morning dress and evening dress, both with large bustles* (1889)

142. *Dresses with trains, even for tennis* (1878)

Dresses were trimmed with frills and flounces and ribbon bows and lace and flowers. This is from a magazine article of the time:

> "Dressmakers load their work with ugly and senseless frills which do not end anything, with bows which do not tie anything and with buttons which are of no use. . . . A dress is considered a perfect fit when a lady can neither raise her arms nor use her legs."

143. *The lady in this group is wearing a dolman. The boys wear sailor suits and the girls' dresses are smaller versions of grown-up styles* (1879)

Notice that even the tennis players in picture 142 have frills and bows.

All the colours of the rainbow were used for dresses and they were often made up of three or four different materials.

The most popular outdoor garment was the *dolman*, which was a sort of cloak with shawl-like sleeves. The lady in the picture above is wearing one.

144. *Dress with leg of mutton sleeves* (1894)

Hats were at last beginning to be more fashionable than bonnets. Indoor caps were largely given up, although some old ladies wore them to the end of the century, and widows even later.

Hair was now piled up on the head and hung down to the back of the neck. A few ringlets might fall over the shoulder, especially with evening dress.

4. The practical period (1890 to 1900)

There was a great change in the last ten years of the 19th century. Skirts, though long, were plain and flared. Sleeves were plain or fashionably puffed out above the elbow into what was called the *leg of mutton* sleeve.

During the day the blouse and skirt was now worn, for the first time, by almost everyone.

51

Evening dresses were low necked, some having ballooned elbow sleeves and some being sleeveless. Yellow was a favourite colour.

Three-quarter-length coats began to be worn out of doors as they were easier to walk in.

Women liked boaters and other small hats. They wore their hair in a fringe or brushed it straight back to a bun behind or on top of the head.

There was a surprising vogue for laced or buttoned boots on all occasions.

Stockings were black, although white stockings were sometimes worn in the summer. Silk evening stockings might be coloured to match the evening dress but black was again usual.

145. *Evening dress with ballooned sleeves* (1893)

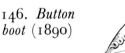

146. *Button boot* (1890)

147. *Lady's bicycling costume* (1895)

Make-up with rouge was practised, but not very much, and well-bred ladies had to be careful that it was not obvious. One day a young girl with a good complexion was stared at while walking down the street by an impertinent young man who remarked: "Painted, by Jove!". She answered quietly, "No Sir, by God".

The move towards clothes more suitable for exercise and sport finally resulted in the most startling costume of the century, the "rational dress". This was the lady's bicycling costume. For the first time she wore *knickerbockers* instead of a skirt. Her legs were free at last, and so, in a short coat with a small felt hat on her head, she cycled gaily into the next century.

149. *Skeleton suit (about 1800–1805)*

148. *Boy aged three in frock and matching "trousers" (1822)*

CHILDREN'S COSTUME

Little boys were dressed like girls up to the age of about four, as you can see in picture 148. They were then put into trousers.

In the early part of the century the trousers were generally buttoned on to a short coat and the two together were called a *skeleton suit*.

Later in the century boys wore knickerbockers, sailor suits or short Eton jackets.

150. *Boy wearing knicker-bockers* (1872)

151. *Sailor suit* (1890)

152. *Eton jacket* (1880's)

Except that they were shorter, the dresses of little girls more or less followed the pattern of their mother's dresses.

154. *Outdoor dress.* a. *Velvet paletot (three-quarter length cloak) and little bonnet* (1852)

b. *Coat with cape, fur-trimmed, for a girl of 7–10 years* (1885)

153a. *Boy in tunic and trousers.* b. *and* c. *Girls wearing long frilled drawers reaching to ankles (about 1840)*

A very inconvenient fashion was the wearing of long white frilled drawers showing below the frock. In fact, uncomfortable and unsuitable clothes went on being worn. However, matters improved a little in the 1890's, as you will see from picture 155.

155. *Girls in short skirts* (1895)

54

156. *Frock coat* (1913)

157. *Morning coat* (1913)

158. *Jacket, trousers with bottoms turned up, bowler hat* (1914)

MEN'S COSTUME

Men's fashions did not alter very much until after the First World War (1914–1918). Trousers were made narrower and though the bottoms were sometimes turned up in the 1890's, by 1912 this was the rule for all.

The frock coat was being replaced by the morning coat for town wear and was worn with a top hat and spats.

A man's ordinary suit consisted of a short jacket, waistcoat and trousers. In 1927 very wide trousers, known as "Oxford bags", were introduced. These measured 22 inches round the bottom of the leg or even 30 inches in their extreme form.

In 1925 men began to wear for golf, and later as casual wear, knickerbockers called *plus-fours*. These were very full and pouched below the knee.

159. *Plus-fours in check tweed* (1928)

The Fair Isle pullover was popular for countrywear as it gave a bit of colour to men's clothes. It was a jersey knitted in coloured designs.

Out of doors, loose overcoats were usual. In town the bowler hat was replacing the top hat but the top hat never went out of fashion for grand occasions. The felt *trilby*, which first came into fashion at the end of the 19th century, became more and more popular.

Gradually men's dress became much less formal, and many stopped wearing waistcoats, hats and gloves even in town. Shoes replaced boots for outdoor wear. Formal costume for special occasions was now often hired.

160. *Overcoat (1910)*

161. *Belted overcoat and trilby hat* (1936)

162. *Motor-cyclist of* 1916 *with dustcoat, leggings, peaked cap and goggles*

163. *Tweed jacket, open-necked shirt and flannel trousers* (1936)

WOMEN'S COSTUME

For the first ten years of this century women wore skirts which swept the ground. Often the skirts had trains which had to be held up when one was walking along muddy roads.

For outdoor wear three-quarter-length or short coats were usual. Either very large hats or toques were fashionable. A *toque* was a hat without a brim or with a close upturned brim. The lady in picture 166 is wearing one.

Next followed a period when walking became still more difficult. The dress with what was called a *hobble skirt* became the fashion. This, too, was long to the ankles and so tight all the way down that stepping on to a bus was almost impossible.

164. *Walking dresses with trains. Large hats* (1902)

165. *This picture pokes fun at hobble skirts. Notice the ladies' large hats* (1911)

166. *Three-quarter length coat and toque* (1901)

During the First World War women had to be active, and the hobble skirt vanished, being replaced by wide skirts. The matching "coat and skirt" of today was adopted by almost everyone.

The most startling change happened from about 1925–1928 when every woman, young and old, took to straight-down dresses, short to the knees and with the waistline round the hips as you can see below.

168a. Short skirt, low waist, cloche hat (1928)

168b. Evening dress (1928)

167a. Coat and skirt (1917). b. Dress with pleated wide skirt (1917)

The popular hat was the *cloche*. It was small, fitting well down over the head, and indeed almost covering the eyes. With this fashion the hair was bobbed, that is, cut very short.

By now black stockings were no longer liked; women preferred them flesh coloured.

Make-up, including lipstick, was used by most young people. In 1927, someone described the girl of this period as

"a curious pinkish legged creature with a scarlet mouth, no waist and almost no hair".

After that, skirts grew longer but, except in evening dresses, they never touched the ground.

Evening dresses, too, were short in front, some longer at the back, and sleeveless.

Then, in the 1930's, what seemed a strange thing happened; women began to wear trousers. They could wear flannel *slacks* in the country and for the first time *shorts* for tennis.

During the years of the Second World War (1939–1945) the real fashion was to be unfashionable. Women wore anything they had that was suitable for their work, and trousers were more and more popular. Trousers, indeed, came to stay and turned into the slacks, jeans and tights of the present day.

169. *Shorts* (1938)

170. *Flannel slacks* (1938)

After the war for a short time there was a violent reaction among girls in favour of a feminine appearance, which was hailed as the "New Look". Dresses and coats were longer, fitted to the waist and widely flared. The hair hung in curls over the collar or was coiled up in a bun.

Soon, however, skirts again became tighter and much shorter, and in recent years fashionable women have shown their knees—perhaps for the first time in English history.

171. *Dress in the style of the "New Look"* (1949)

59

CHILDREN'S COSTUME

Except perhaps for the popular "sailor suit", worn by both boys and girls, in Edwardian days children's clothes were still what we should call uncomfortable. Small boys at many schools had to wear, every Sunday, a tight jacket, a deep stiffly starched white "Eton" collar, and a hard straw hat or *topper* (top hat).

172. Girl in outdoor costume (1901)

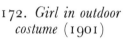

173. Girl's sailor blouse (1900)

174. Boy in Eton suit (1901)

Little girls often had fussy frocks, white pinafores and boots, and they nearly always had to wear hats out of doors.

Girls' stockings were made of black wool which had two horrible qualities. Their dye came off on the feet and every single week they had to be darned.

175. Boy in sailor suit. Girls wear white frocks and black stockings. One is wearing boots (1910)

For the next forty years the story becomes a more cheerful one. Formal clothes were less and less worn by boys. Girls were allowed simple frocks and finally shorts or jeans for everyday, or even play-suits. Clothes at last were designed for freedom and comfort as well as for looks. But what a time it had taken!

177. *Boy in woollen jersey, shorts* (1929)

176. *Simple cotton dress, hair ribbon* (1930)

178. *Girl in shorts* (1932)

179. *Playsuits* (1934)

After having read about so many changes in fashion through some thousand years of English history, I wonder if you will agree with William Mason, who wrote in 1782: "Fashion ever is a wayward child."

SOME FASHIONS OF THE 1980's

MUSEUMS IN BRITAIN WITH COSTUME
COLLECTIONS

BATH   Museum of Costume, Assembly Rooms

BELFAST   Museum and Art Gallery

BIRMINGHAM   City Museum and Art Gallery

BRISTOL   Blaise Castle Folk Museum

CARDIFF   Welsh Folk Museum, St. Fagans

CHELTENHAM   Art Gallery and Museum

COLCHESTER   Castle Museum, Holly Trees Annexe

DOUGLAS, ISLE OF MAN   Manx Museum

EDINBURGH   Royal Scottish Museum and National Museum of Antiquities of
   Scotland

EXETER   Royal Albert Memorial Museum

GLASGOW   Art Gallery and Museum

HALIFAX Bankfield Museum

HEREFORD City Museum and Art Gallery

IPSWICH Christchurch Mansion

LEEDS City Museum

      Temple Newsam House

LEICESTER Museum and Art Gallery

LONDON Victoria and Albert Museum

      Bethnal Green Museum

      London Museum

LUTON Museum and Art Gallery

MAIDSTONE Museum and Art Gallery

MANCHESTER Gallery of English Costume,
      Platt Hall

NORTHAMPTON Museum and Art Gallery

NORWICH Castle Museum

NOTTINGHAM Castle Museum

PRESTON Harris Museum and Art Gallery

SALISBURY Salisbury, South Wilts. and Blackmore Museum

TAUNTON Somerset County Museum

WORTHING Museum and Art Gallery

YORK Castle Museum

      Castle Howard, Costume Galleries

Lady in riding habit
(1720)

MORE BOOKS FOR YOU TO READ

Bradfield, N, *Historical Costumes of England 1066–1956* (3rd edition), Harrap
Crush, Margaret, *Costume*, Franklin Watts, First Look At Series, 1972
Cunnington, Phillis and Buck, Anne, *Children's Costume in England*, A & C Black, 1965
Fox, Lilla M, *Costume*, Transworld, How and Why Series, 1975
Healey, T M, *History of Costume*, Macdonald Education, 1977
Laver, James, *Concise History of Costume*, Thames and Hudson, 1969
Yarwood, Doreen, *Outline of English Costume*, Batsford, 1967

BOOKS FOR REFERENCE

Five separate Handbooks on English Costume, one for each of the periods Medieval, 16th, 17th, 18th and 19th Centuries, written by C. W. and P. Cunnington, are published by Messrs. Faber & Faber.

INDEX

This index will help you to find things quickly. The numbers are page numbers.